*On Life, Love,
Literature
& Letter Writing*

On Life, Love, Literature & Letter Writing
By Christine Yunn-Yu Sun

First published in February 2015. This edition published in 2018
by eBook Dynasty, an imprint of Solid Software Pty Ltd.
P.O. Box 218, Belgrave, Victoria 3160, Australia

Web: http://www.ebookdynasty.net/index.html
Email: contact@ebookdynasty.net

© Christine Yunn-Yu Sun 2015, 2018

This book is copyright. Except for private study, research, criticism
or review, as permitted under the Copyright Act, no part of this book
may be reproduced, stored in a retrieval system, or transmitted
in any form by any means without proper written permission.
Enquiries should be made to the publisher.

Cover design by Christine Yunn-Yu Sun
Typeset by eBook Dynasty
"Independence in Writing, Freedom in Publishing."

On Life, Love, Literature & Letter Writing

For D and S

Index

#1:	Letter-Writing Nostalgia	6
#2:	National Dreams	9
#3:	Identity and Writing	11
#4:	A Room of One's Own	14
#5:	On "Freedom"	17
#6:	On Decluttering	20
#7:	Childhood's End	22
#8:	In Love with Sherlock	24
#9:	Ambitions and Opportunities	27
#10:	Life in a Brand New World	29
#11:	On Depression	32
#12:	Chance Encounters	36
#13:	A Change of Scenery	39
#14:	Book Giving	42
#15:	Being a Migrant	45
#16:	Searching for the Past	48
#17:	Law and Literature	52
#18:	Life Writing and Sharing	55
#19:	Modern-day Letter Writing	58
#20:	Reading Friends from Afar	60
#21:	Life in Other Lands	64
#22:	One Letter at a Time	67
#23:	Letter-Writing "Celebrities"?	70
#24:	Dealing with Rejections	76
#25:	Hands in Friendship	79

#26:	On Constructive Criticism	82
#27:	On "Uneven Ink"	85
#28:	The Power of Words	88
(#29:	Pretending It's a Leap Year)	87

On Life, Love, Literature & Letter Writing

#1: Letter-Writing Nostalgia

February 1, 2015
To: A.L., Taipei, Taiwan

Dear A,

Greetings from Australia. This is my first InCoWriMo – a big challenge. To me, writing is easy, and I am more than happy to write everyday. However, writing by hand is difficult, for I have been writing with computers since my teenage years and my handwriting is lousy as a result. I guess you can see this already. :)

Still, I want to challenge myself to write by hand everyday for a whole month, for three reasons. Firstly, this seems to be a "writerly" thing to do, a romantic and even nostalgic way to continue the good old literary tradition of writing on paper, in the same way that reading and printing on paper are nowadays still cherished. As an avid reader as well as a publisher of Chinese ebooks, I am perfectly aware of the fact that paper will never die – despite the fact that many trees have died and will continue to die for this. As the renowned Italian novelist and scholar Umberto Eco said in his 2003 essay "Vegetal and mineral memory: The future of books" – once we understand "what we usually mean by book, text, literature, interpretation, and so on", it becomes obvious why questions such as "Will the new electronic media make books obsolete?" are silly.

Secondly, keeping a journal is certainly helpful for a writingcareer. It even benefits one's translation from one language to another, which is what I do most of the time these days. Translation is another form of creative writing, for one has to re-present the thoughts and feelings of others as faithfully, fluently and gracefully as possible. ("The truth, the whole truth and nothing but the truth, so help me God.") Furthermore, as they "crawl through" the writing one word at a time, translators also act as editors and proofreaders who often catch the writers and publishers off guard. Finally and most importantly, translation as a profession helps to inspire those translators who dream of also being writers. Such inspiration needs recording in the form of a journal before it fades into oblivion as translators move on to the next project.

Finally, writing, particularly letter writing, enables people to be spiritually closer to each other even when they are physically miles apart. I, for one, suffer from a kind of loneliness that is only to be found in today's Internet age. Among the torrents of information we consume everyday, there is hardly a soul that echoes ours and uplifts us beyond our existing dreams and desires. Indeed, apart from tons of words, images and sounds, one would be lucky to find a soul in cyberspace. We are merely dots of nameless dust being blown this way and that by the great trending (or trading?) winds of the World Wide Web.

Letter writing, on the other hand, encourages us to reflect upon our lives – our ideals and pursuits, our voices and unvoiced longings, our silence. By transforming our daily musings into words on paper, we confirm our existence. Even better, by recording our existence and sending it out to someone – even a stranger – we find a purpose. Meanwhile, our decision on what and what not to share with the others helps me to sort out how and how much we will let our purpose impact on our existence.

That is enough rambling. Here is something I found in today's reading, to share with you. It is a writer's representation of an African tribal man's views about reading and writing.

"It was absurd, he knew, but he was wary of anyone who could read and write... He was not sure whether to regard them as normal people or as witchdoctors who could cast spells."

Yours Sincerely,
Christine

#2: National Dreams

February 2, 2015
To: E.S., Highland, California, U.S.A.

Dear E,

Greetings from Australia. Thank you for updating your address in California so that this letter will reach you sooner than taking a detour to Mexico. I assume you are doing research between the two countries, but please correct me if I am wrong. Usually I would assume it is a pleasure to constantly travel, but I would like to hear your views on the similarities and differences between American and Mexican cultures.

I would also like to ask how you started InCoWriMo. It is a fascinating international event, and I am sure you find the experience rewarding. Throughout the years I have seen various campaigns online promoting a similar cause, but many of them seem to attract only people in the United States. On the other hand, the Americans have plenty of national events that are now worldwide celebrations of writing and reading. For instance, are you a supporter of the International Book Giving Day on February 14?

Having experienced both American and Australian cultures, I find the American Dream being much more ambitious, competitive and even fierce than the Australian Dream. I often think of the 2000 Sydney Olympics whose opening ceremony showcased great Aussie icons such as the Hills Hoist (a height-adjustable rotary clothes line), the Victa lawn mower and a pair of gigantic thongs. (Not the UGG boots, thank you very much.) Many of my family members and friends are content with a mortgage-free house and a huge backyard where they can barbecue, swim and party whenever they like. In this sense, a plumber can be much richer and happier than a bank manager or leader of a huge business corporation.

It is even more eye-opening for me, who came from a Chinese background (not China but Taiwan), to experience a life that focuses more on well-earned leisure than desperate hard work. The Chinese are great survivors, in my view. They can and are willing to do anything and everything just to get ahead of the others. Such a sense of (sometimes blindly) dashing ahead is further boosted by the so-called "Chinese Dream" promoted by their government, whose aim is to stand shoulder-to-shoulder with the "West", i.e. the United States. This is despite the fact that the West is such a diverse environment with many different cultures, each featuring a unique ideology and lifestyle.

What do you think? I look forward to hearing from you.

Yours Sincerely,

Christine

#3: Identity and Writing

February 3, 2015
To: S.K., Singapore

Dear S,

Greetings from Australia. Thank you for adding me to your list of international correspondents. It is a pleasure to meet someone from Singapore, even just through letter writing.

I have been to Singapore only once, when I was little. Throughout the years since, I have read a lot of books about its history and culture, including the novels of several Singaporean Chinese and Eurasian authors. One of my good friends currently lives there.

But it is impossible to really know a country, unless your family has lived there for generations and witnessed all the socio-political and cultural changes. Our impression of anything and everything only derives from our concrete experience of them, including all the relevant information we have absorbed from our family, school and the media. Other than that, there is hardly anything else.

For instance, I often find my knowledge about a certain country is limited. What I know from books, movies and the Internet is definitely not enough, so I have learned to be extremely cautious when commenting on anything and everything about other people's affairs. Obviously I make mistakes, but I get my precious lessons from them. It is amazing how patient and tolerant people can be about my ignorance.

I guess a sense of awe and the wide-eyed fascinated look on my face always helps. :)

I have studied issues of cultural identity and how we are identified not only by the others but also by ourselves. Particularly for writers, there can be a considerable difference between how they view themselves and how their readers (and critics) think of them and their books. Now that I am writing to you, again I recall the kind of Singapore portrayed in the novels of various writers from there. I am curious to know what you think, as your views of your country will definitely be different from the common stereotypes people have about it.

Here is something I came upon last night, to share with you. I do not necessarily agree with it, but I think it is interesting to explore why such a view came into existence. It is from a fellow writer who can find neither a genre nor a place for her writings to "fit in", i.e. getting published:

"I have…researched numerous online journals and literary magazines in the hope of finding one (at least) in which my poetry would fit. I managed to find 5 or 6, but they were not a perfect fit as it turned out because I was rejected on the grounds of 'not fitting in'."

"I then turned my attention to my novel. I scrutinised 50+ small presses, and a handful of traditional publishers, in Australia, with the aim of submitting my book for consideration (when it was ready). This research presented a new problem of 'not fitting in'. I wasn't an Australian writer – I was displaced. I had no national identity to claim or cling to. All of the publishers and guidelines mentioned the words 'Australian writers' and 'Australian-themed stories' as a prerequisite. It wasn't much different abroad either – a writer's national identity is equally important as their publication history or the genre they write. When it became clear that my work would not 'fit' within publishers in general, I knew that it was time to think outside of the box and find a solution."

I would like to know your view. Do you think we can eventually rise above our (national and other) identities to achieve our goal, if not in writing, then in other aspects of our life?

Yours Sincerely,
Christine

#4: A Room of One's Own

February 4, 2015
To: C.L.D., Olive Hill, Kentucky, U.S.A.

Dear C,

Greetings from Australia. Since I started InCoWriMo at the beginning of this month, this is the first time I find it difficult to pen a letter. You will have to pardon me if my words below are not very coherent.

Today (Wednesday) I spent the whole day cooking, in preparation for a party on Saturday. I made chicken sausage rolls, chicken nuggets and chicken dumplings (we love chicken in this house), and will make more dishes tomorrow and the day after that.

As a writer and translator who works in a home-office, I have no excuse to splash money outside of the house for the simple pleasure of dining and wining. Throughout the years I have developed quite a repertoire, and can easily cook for a crowd of up to 40 people, in either Chinese or Western style. No trouble. It only costs me plenty of time. To borrow a common Chinese saying, "Even the most talented housewife cannot cook without time." (The original saying involves rice.)

However, time is expensive, and it is the only thing that once lost will never come back. My work suffers greatly as I spend time cooking, for even though I am happy to cook, I cannot do writing or translation at the same time. I can hardly think – my mind gets lost as I wander among the stove, the oven, the sink, the fridge and the pantry.

On Life, Love, Literature & Letter Writing

My head becomes increasingly empty as my hands get busy.

Perhaps this is why a lot of female writers support the view that women need to have "a room of their own". I suspect these words, first expressed by Virginia Woolf in 1929 in a lecture titled "A Room of One's Own", do not merely indicate a physical space in real life where women can be alone and not bothered by house affairs. More than that, I think the "room" here conveys a sense of intellectual independence and solitude that women have been seeking since the beginning of time. A woman needs to be eccentric, selfish, stubborn and even arrogant from time to time, if only in this aspect of her life. It helps her to recognise her value as a person.

Woolf was asked to speak about women and fiction. In her words: "This might mean women and what they are like, or it might mean women and the fiction that they write; or it might mean women and the fiction that is written about them, or it might mean that somehow all three are inextricably mixed together." Considering the very last possibility, she came up with this personal opinion:

"A woman must have money and a room of her own if she is to write fiction; and that...leaves the great problem of the true nature of woman and the true nature of fiction unsolved."

I find it interesting that people, particularly women, rarely quote the second half of this sentence. Indeed, if a woman does not know herself, intellectually, then neither a room of her own nor money can help her find out where she stands in literary and other senses.

If a woman does not have the courage to discover and pursue what she really wants, intellectually, then I suspect no amount of feminism can help to solve her problems in life. On the contrary, if a woman understands who she is and what she wants to do for her future, then I am sure no amount of sexism can hinder her success.

    I would like to know what you think. Do you have a room of your own?

Yours Sincerely,
Christine

On Life, Love, Literature & Letter Writing

#5: On "Freedom"

February 5, 2015
To: A.N., San Quentin, California, U.S.A.

Dear A,

Greetings from Australia. Sorry that I have not written to you for more than two years. I wonder if you still remember me? I kind of hope that you are still there to receive this letter. However, I also hope you are no longer there – that you have left "in a good way" and are now pursuing a happy life somewhere out there.

The past two years have been very tough for me, which is why I did not write. I want my letters to bring you happy thoughts, but I guess any news is better than no news. Sorry.

This evening I saw an interview on television, about an Australian journalist called Peter Greste, who had just arrived home after being imprisoned in Egypt for 400 days. He and two colleagues were reporting on various events when they were arrested and accused of helping the terrorists in that country. Without people worldwide continuously calling for the Egyptian Government to release him, he would have been sentenced to seven years in jail.

On television they showed footage of his happy reunion with family, friends and colleagues, who have been tirelessly calling for every individual, group, society and government they could think of to help. They also showed a photograph of him standing knee-deep in water on the beach of Cyprus, as a stopover during his long flight from

Egypt back to Australia. On his face was the biggest smile I have ever seen on anybody. He said it felt incredibly good after 400 days of imprisonment, 400 dark nights of always wondering whether there would be a light at the end of the tunnel, always worrying how his loved ones would cope, yet always trying to maintain positive and strong. Obviously he associates freedom with the blue sky, the sandy beach and the green, vast ocean. After all, he is an Aussie.

I used to associate freedom with birds, back in my youthful days when words such as "worry" and "sorrow" made no sense. To me, back then, the word "freedom" was taken for granted. It was an existence so "natural" that no one bothered to find out who did and did not have it and why. However, as time went by, I slowly came to realise that "freedom" exists as a concept only when it ceases to exist. People will never know what "freedom" is unless they have experienced its loss, emotionally, physically, intellectually, or even spiritually.

I am not saying I completely understand how you feel. Indeed, I practically know nothing at all about your life there. Still, even though I have not been writing, I think of you often and every time I do so I wish you a tiny bit of joy, peace and warmth in a place so full of fury, chaos and hostility. I wish you a glimpse of light on the dark side of the moon.

I will continue to write, in the hope that you will eventually forgive me and start responding again. Even better, I hope that one day you will write to me from a different address – something that seems unlikely but never absolutely impossible.

Please take care. I look forward to hearing from you.

On Life, Love, Literature & Letter Writing

Yours Sincerely,
Christine

#6: On Decluttering

February 6, 2015
To: L.N., Chatham, Ontario, Canada

Dear L,

Greetings from Australia. I am writing a short note to you tonight because we have just spent the whole day cleaning the house. It is exhausting work. Yet, because we only tidy up the house whenever there is a party coming up (which is not very often), once it is done it is actually quite satisfying.

I once saw this quote, "You never know what you have until you clean your room." It is so true. I often discover books that I think are long lost, and it feels like having received a new book for free. It feels even better when I finally find a book I need to quote from, in the corner of a dusty room or somewhere under a pile of junk, after a long day of searching high and low. Rejoice! The writing lives to see another day!

I suspect this is why we enjoy travelling – holiday accommodations are always attractive because they are much tidier than home. Less furniture, less junk, less things to wash and clean. Then I can have more time to appreciate whatever there is in front of me. Less cluttering means there is more empty space for me to roam around, both emotionally and intellectually. No wonder I never like "Where's Wally?" sort of books.

I like this quote by Louise Smith even better, "You can't reach for anything new if your hands are still full of yesterday's junk." The only exception is perhaps with books, for I never abandon them. It physically hurts me whenever I see people throwing away perfectly fine books. It is like capital punishment, which completely denies the value of life. A light at the end of the tunnel is shut down because people are tired of always searching for new possibilities and adventures.

Decluttering is a game, an exercise of the mind, to explore, investigate, analyse and prioritise, then to re-organise, re-discover, re-experience and re-enjoy. Having sorted out what to keep and what to send away as pre-loved goods, we now can start the cluttering process all over again. How wonderful life is!

Yours Sincerely,
Christine

#7: Childhood's End

February 7, 2015
To: S.L., Coquitlam, British Columbia, Canada

Dear S,

Greetings from Australia. It was party time here today, with people coming and going and up to seven kids running and screaming in and outside of the house the whole day. The hot and humid weather did not help, but seeing the birthday girl's smiling face makes it all worthwhile.

Again I cooked too much – chicken nuggets, chicken sausage rolls, vegetarian sausage rolls, pork dumplings, green onion cakes, salmon quiches, mushroom quiches, basil pesto pizza, garlic and parsley pizza, seafood sushi, vegetarian sushi, fairy bread, two types of chocolate cake, and a whole lot of nibbles and drinks. It is lucky that we love leftovers.

Doing birthday parties for kids always reminds me of the science fiction novel *Childhood's End*, published in 1953. I have never read it, but it is Arthur C. Clarke's own favourite novel and has always been considered "a classic of alien literature". While the concept of apparent utopia at the cost of one's identity and culture is attractive, the title itself fascinates me. It symbolises the end of innocence, the conclusion of pure, happy, worry-free feelings and dreams. The lolly shop is shut, its curtains drawn and neon signs turned off. There is no turning back after this.

What happens next is serious intellectual thinking, idealism and ideologies, goals and pursuits, responsibilities and obligations, passion, jealousy, sorrow, love and hatred. Adulthood is not a bright and blissful period of time — we are simply too busy to enjoy anything. The library is open and we are lost in it. In order to search for a light, we need to first create darkness. It is as boring as those "muffin movers" — simple old containers dressed up as fashionable items for posh new-age commuters who have money to burn.

Still, as everybody sat there, filled with all sorts of food and drink, sweating even in the shade, like a group of beached whales so close yet so far away from the cool ocean – life went on. When the house was finally quiet, we were all exhausted. It would be another dreamless night, then the next day would be back to normal.

Do you like parties?

Yours Sincerely,

Christine

On Life, Love, Literature & Letter Writing

#8: In Love with Sherlock

February 8, 2015
To: M.K.R., Dundee, U.K.

Dear M,

Greetings from Australia. Do you watch much television? These days I have been a faithful viewer of *Sherlock*, the immensely popular BBC series that is now filming its Season 4 in England. Here in Australia we only started Season 1 at the beginning of this year, but I am already hooked.

I have always been fascinated by the idea of Time. It started out as a vague awareness, when I began to read bilingually, of the difference between the publishing time of an English-language book and that of its Chinese edition. Take the Harry Potter books as an example. When all the kids and their parents were waiting patiently outside bookstores across the English world for the sales of the books to begin, such frenzy did not reach the Chinese world until several months or even more than a year later, when the books were finally translated into Chinese. Even the Chinese media did not report much on the stunning popularity of these books in the West, for they knew it would not make much sense to most of the Chinese audience who do not read English.

Things are a little bit better now. Publishers in the Chinese world have learned to grab the Traditional or Simplified Chinese rights ahead of schedule, at international book fairs and through all sorts of literary agencies, so that when the English-language books are published, their Chinese editions are not far behind. For example, when the authorised biography of Steve Jobs was published in October 2011, the publisher of its Traditional Chinese edition somehow managed to have purchased the rights half a year earlier. Their three translators worked desperately for four months to enable the Traditional Chinese edition to be launched in Taiwan on the same day as the English original came out. It was truly a ground-breaking effort. As for the Simplified Chinese edition, the publisher in China simply picked the easy way and converted everything from the Traditional Chinese edition.

Still, Time is fascinating because, even though you get to read a book years after everybody else has read and talked about it, to you it is still the first time. It is still like the first time you fall in love, when everything is new and colourful, full of endless sweetness and unnecessary sorrow, mixed with a bit of jealousy and doubt, but mainly a sense of awe and wonder. You feel forever young. The memory is etched deep in your mind, and the love lasts forever.

In recent months I had a chance to watch the five Twilight movies, as well as the three Stieg Larsson films in Swedish. I also got to read David Mitchell's *Cloud Atlas* and Harper Lee's *To Kill a Mockingbird* for the first time. People have long consumed these works and repeatedly examined them, but the same fascination about Time always exists, so much so that I still fully immersed myself in them. Now I feel I am in love with Sherlock Holmes, in English, in a audio-visual way – and it is a love that is completely different from what I felt reading the Chinese editions of Sir Conan Doyle's books some 30 years ago!

Perhaps my next InCoWriMo letter should be to the Australian Broadcasting Corporation (ABC), demanding them – begging them, on my knees! – to start showing Season 2 of *Sherlock* as soon as possible. What else can you do when you are lovesick?

Yours Sincerely,
Christine

On Life, Love, Literature & Letter Writing

#9: Ambitions and Opportunities

February 9, 2015
To: M.G., Pawleys Island, South Carolina, U.S.A.

Dear M,

Greetings from Australia. Glad to meet you on paper via InCoWriMo 2015. What do you do as a career? If you have already retired, what used to be your job?

I have a series of professional titles, but the ones I use most often are "bilingual writer" and "translator". These days I do more translation work than writing, because I have made promises to people who rely on my skills to fulfil their dreams. I love translating literary titles, although there is also plenty of work for non-literary projects.

But I love writing even better. Particularly when I get to have some time to write my own stuff – which is rare – it feels like staggering into an oasis after crossing a whole desert. Here the water is cool and fresh, the shade pleasant and the dates so tender and juicy they nearly melt in your mouth. You climb down from the camel's back and move towards a lake, ready to swim, splash and splatter in words. Eventually you fall asleep on the green grass by the water, dreaming about your words growing wings to fly you far, far away.

The beginning of each year seems to be full of opportunities. Everyday I see grants and funding to apply for, contests and competitions to enter, conferences and journals calling for papers, proposals and presentations – windows of all shapes and sizes that potentially open to a brand new piece of blue sky. Facing all these possible chances, which may lead to dramatic changes in life, how do you suppress your ambitions? How can you not dream large? Most importantly, how do you refrain your imagination from going wild, so that you can concentrate on the tasks at hand? How do you stop daydreaming?

Today I saw this quote from one of the books I have translated from English to Chinese. "The movie-makers have some bright ideas. They have great imaginations and they have all the tools, but they still rely on facts. Moreover, they have the sense to hire expert advisers who keep them within the bounds of reality."

Well, the lesson I learned from this quote is that every daydreamer needs to have at least one expert adviser to keep their feet firmly on the ground. To help them remain "within the bounds of reality" and focus on the tasks they are already facing. To encourage and even force them to fulfil their promises. Perhaps more importantly, every daydreamer needs to have a "devil" on their left shoulder (or the right one if it suits them better) that keeps warning them off all the sidetracks. "Do you really think you can handle all that extra work? Why don't you just stick to your own stuff and leave the opportunities to other (more) talented people? To hell with your crazy ambitions!"

Finish one thing before starting on the next. This is my lesson. I would be very grateful for your advice in this regard.

Yours Sincerely,

Christine

#10: Life in a Brand New World

February 10, 2015
To: R, c/o J.G., Boulder, Colorado, U.S.A.

Dear R,

Greetings from Australia. I found your contact details, via J.G., on the website of More Love Letters. They suggest it is a good idea to write something nice to help you survive life in the strange new world that is New York City, so here I am. I hope my writing can bring you some comfort.

I have only been to NYC twice, both times as a tourist. It does not fascinate me in the same way that many other American cities and towns do, but I do understand why so many people go there to set up a new life and end up feeling unease and totally alone. To me, it is not the city that terrorises the newly arrived. It is the unknown future stretching ahead of them until forever.

When I studied and lived in the United States it was in Columbus, Ohio. A university town lacking glamour, fashion and class, I suppose, but it was still a brand new place to me, an international student whose first language is not even English. Mind you, it took me nearly a year to start dreaming in English. I think it signified an acceptance and appreciation of my life in that language – I had finally settled down.

That first year was lonely, yes, because I was experiencing two shocks, one in culture and the other in language. I spent a lot of time reading, sleeping and dreaming, trying to hold onto everything familiar, but also forcing myself to embrace something new everyday. I was trying to conquer my stereotypes about the American culture, while also confronting various misconceptions the American people have about my culture. I think the former is harder to do.

I think there is a general confusion between loneliness and solitude, particularly when you are completely alone for the first time. There are people everywhere, but none of them understands you, at least not from the beginning. You also think there is no one to trust, but this does not mean they are not worthy of it. As a common Chinese saying goes, a journey of a thousand miles starts at the first step.

I started enjoying my solitude in a brand new city by familiarising myself with people who appeared to be trustworthy – people working in supermarkets, staff at bookstores, librarians, etc. Because they were always there, I saw them as living landmarks highlighting the humane side of the place. I took long walks whenever I could, just to see how shops and houses slowly transformed in time. Give it two weeks. Use yourself as a yardstick to measure how much people can change. Then you will realise how much you are changing as well.

I also started participating in activities organised by local groups and libraries. There are plenty of people out there who dedicate their lives to helping others. There is no need to talk to them – all you have to do is to observe their facial expressions and actions to know their hearts are gentle and kind. After a while you will realise it is not hard to build up courage to become part of them. I did this, and ended up having fierce debates with a group of Christian friends on what is "the Truth, the whole Truth and nothing but the Truth". It was a lot of fun. Trust me, people will only debate with you when they know and appreciate your intelligence.

Most of all, I would say the best way to truly know a place is to read about it. Do you enjoy reading? Both loneliness and solitude are helpful in developing a thirst for books. Go to your local library and ask about novels based on the history of NYC. A lot of them would be about migrants, such as Beverly Swerling's *City of Dreams* and Kevin Baker's *Dreamland*. If you like the classics, then F. Scott Fitzgerald's *The Great Gatsby* and Betty Smith's *A Tree Grows in Brooklyn* will do. (Personally, I enjoy Ira Levin's *Rosemary's Baby* and Stephen King's *The Stand*, but horror is really an acquired taste and in this case may not suit your needs. I am completely ignorant with romance novels. Sorry.)

What I really want to say is, get to know the city a little bit at a time, and use that as your foundation to seek and find more. Make yourself belong to the city so that it will belong to you. It is the same with ideals and goals – what you set out to do will eventually come to you, but you can help it arrive faster by going towards it. I wish you all the best.

Yours Sincerely,

Christine

#11: On Depression

February 11, 2015
To: A, c/o P.J., London, Ontario, Canada

Dear A,

Greetings from Australia. I saw information about you, via your sister P., on the website of More Love Letters. It says you recently gave birth to a lovely little baby girl – *congratulations!* – but you were diagnosed with postnatal depression. It triggered something in my heart, so I decided to write a letter and share a bit of my own experience with you. I hope you do not mind.

I, too, have been through that dark tunnel. Indeed, I saw a quote today that perfectly describes such an experience: "When you struggle with something like depression or anxiety or both, your brain isn't functioning normally on any level. You really believe the terrible things your mind is telling you."

The person who wrote this went on to say: "Someone told me that there comes a grieving period when depression/anti-anxiety medication and/or therapy and/or other treatment starts to really work. It's not grieving about losing who you are; it's about how much you denied your past self. About how you didn't give yourself the chance to function but listened to those painful messages your mind fed you."

According to P, you really want to know whether there would

be a light at the end of the tunnel. My answer is YES, that light is always there and will never go away, although the tunnel is very long, much longer than you think, so long that you almost want to believe that it will never end. The second part of my answer is YES, YOU CAN AND WILL reach the end of the tunnel and find that light. There is no doubt about it.

Beyond the tunnel, you WILL find that blue sky. I am sorry to say that you will have to do this all by yourself, that no one else can help you. However, it definitely helps to know that other people are going through their own tunnels as well. You are not alone, because we are alone *together*.

I was lucky to have fulfilled some of my life's dreams before my first child was born. However, as I sat there with my baby at home, day in and day out, feeling completely exhausted, physically, emotionally and intellectually, I, too, wondered whether all of this would ever end. It was a sense of loss, of Self, that depressed me. Life went on, the whole world moved on, people continued to do whatever they had been doing, only I was stuck there, frozen in time and action, completely on my own, like a mannequin in an empty shop, with a crying machine that was operating 24x7. I did not know *who* I was, *what* I was, not to mention *why* I was. Is this how you are feeling now?

I used to feel so frustrated that, despite everyone's kind (offer of) assistance, I was the one who had to face my life. There was no way out, because I was the one who chose to walk down this road. We as women today are free to, and indeed do, make our own choices, and we definitely have enough intelligence and skills to back ourselves up. Still, when we are so tired of being independent, when we feel so weak and vulnerable, so *alone*, we need a rest. We want to just lie down and close our eyes, not to think, see or hear anything, not to be bothered by anybody. We just want our own cocoon that is the tender loving darkness, in which we can find our solitude.

I remember sitting there, staring at nothing outside the window, with tears streaming down my face, feeling completely useless, helpless and hopeless. I remember thinking *there is no way out, at least not in the foreseeable future, and there is nothing I can do about it*. I remember lying down whenever I could, trying to avoid other people's prying and caring eyes, to think of nothing, to pursue and embrace that numbing unconsciousness, to *escape*. There was bright sunlight everywhere, but all I wanted was darkness. Forever.

Then, one day, I was out of it. Just like that. Like waking up after having had enough sleep. There was no struggle, no sense of unbelievable luck, of finally being *free*. It was all very natural, like breathing, like taking one step after another. Only when I looked back did I realise I had completed the tunnel. I was out.

Please trust me, you, too, can and will achieve this. There is no need to feel depressed about your depression, because it will pass, like clouds drifting away from the moon. That moon is always there. You have not lost anything. You still have your Self.

All you need to do is to live one day at a time – live it for yourself and your baby, and live it well. If necessary, live one hour at a time. Focus on your tasks at hand and do them properly. Whenever you get a chance, rest. Whenever people offer to help, let them. You can always thank them later.

Please believe me, this is not the time to be considerate. On the contrary, you should be fiercely selfish and look after yourself, because your baby girl is a part of you. Whatever happens, she will always love you, but she can only be happy when you are. By looking after yourself, you are taking good care of her.

And remember, you are not alone. People do care. *I* care, all the way from the other side of the world, because I know how you feel. The tunnel is long and dark, so what? You, too, can shine on.

Yours Sincerely,

Christine

#12: Chance Encounters

February 12. 2015
To: R.G., Puunene, Hawaii, U.S.A.

Dear R,

Greetings from Australia. I saw in your CFL (Call for Letters) that you expect an interesting story, and that your response will somehow be "unconventional". Well, here is a story for you:

I went to the city today for an interview. Not for any formal job – I already have one – just an voluntary position that I really cared about. As a perfect example of Murphy's Law, I was so keen to get to the city on time that everything that could possibly go wrong did. Horrible traffic jam, a bus driver that was slower than a sloth, a long queue in front of the ticketing machine – you name it. Somehow I managed to step on the train a moment before it started moving.

I did not have time to top up my Myki Card (a "durable, rechargeable smartcard that stores value which can be used as payment for public transport fares", according to its website), so Murphy's Law again proved true and dumped a ticket inspector on me. I nervously explained what happened, apologised profusely and vowed to recharge my card as soon as I got off the train – and he let me go! It was an extremely close call, nearly costing me a fine of 100 dollars!

Meanwhile, a lady sitting directly in front of me was also in trouble. Her problem was worse because she was travelling on Concession Ticket without a valid Concession ID – a really big no-no these days in Melbourne, indeed. Luckily the ticket inspector only issued a warning, instead of sending her straight to court. Still, she was so distraught that her whole body was trembling.

It is worth noting here that our ticket inspector was really polite and reasonable, unlike those power-hungry maniacs we see in the news who are so keen to act like real law-enforcers that they wrestle and even pepper-spray misbehaving passengers to the ground. It was nice to bump into a professional inspector for a change.

Later the lady in front of me made a call on her mobile phone. In the usual fashion that all mobile communications on public transport are loud enough for everybody to hear, she explained to whoever was listening that she had an unfortunate incident on the train but would definitely arrive on time for her job interview. What a coincidence! Like me, she was facing a forthcoming opportunity that could potentially change her life.

I love this kind of chance encounter. When I went to Hawaii for the first and only time in my life, it was back in the summer of 1991, after graduating from high school. I had been studying English as a second language for six years prior to that, but it was only "classroom English" in Taiwan, with no chance to ever use the Lagrange in real life. I soon discovered the problem of this. While attending a series of festive activities on Waikiki Beach with friends, I became overwhelmed by the happily chattering and screaming crowd. Somehow my arm got stuck around a little girl's neck, and there was nothing I could do about it – partly because it was so crowded that no one was able to move an inch, and partly because I could not let go of my friend's hand for the fear of losing my way home.

The little girl was so distraught that she burst into tears. Her mother, a large black lady, glared at me and started yelling at the top of her voice, "Let her go! LET HER GO!" I desperately wanted to tell her that I could not do so, that I, too, feared getting lost in this crazy sea of strange people. But I was unable to convey all of this in English – I did not know how! I could only look at her pleadingly, hoping she could understand how helpless and hopeless I was at that moment!

I have no memory of how the incident ended, but that chance encounter changed my life forever. Since then I have dedicated myself to studying English, not only speaking and listening but also reading and writing. And here I am, a global citizen enjoying the use of English everyday. It is such a fascinating language that the more I know about it, the more I want to embrace it as my own.

Well, I hope you like this story. Now it is your turn – what kind of "unconventional" response will you have for me? I look forward to receiving it.

Yours Sincerely,
Christine

On Life, Love, Literature & Letter Writing

#13: A Change of Scenery

February 13, 2015
To: A.D., Trnava, Slovak Republic

Dear A,

Greetings from Australia. Do you like travelling? How often do you travel outside of your town, city or even country? Or, perhaps you enjoy staying put and having everything going smooth and steady? Either is fine, of course. Everybody is different.

I do not go out very often, so every time I venture outside of the house, I grab the chance to enjoy the change of scenery. I always remember a book I read about, *Alice I Have Been*. Written by American author Melanie Benjamin, this is a fictional account of the life of Alice Liddell, who was Lewis Carroll's inspiration when he wrote the famous children's book *Alice's Adventures in Wonderland*. When I read an interview with Benjamin back in 2010, on how she came to write her book on Alice as a girl and later as a woman, wife and mother, I was so impressed with her words that I copied them down in my journal. Now I copy them here for you.

When asked if she could give some advice to other authors, Benjamin said:

"Open your eyes – get out of the house! I think that authors, very often, get stuck in a rut; they spend their time alone, concentrating on one thing – one story, one novel, one idea – and fixate on it. Some spend years and years reworking the same idea. I was close to being in this place – and then I took the train into Chicago and wandered into a photography exhibit, which changed my life as an artist. Authors need to experience life, and art, and keep their minds – and eyes – open to every possibility. We can't remain chained to our computers all the time."

What Benjamin saw in that exhibit was a series of photographs taken by Carroll, whose real name was Charles Lutwidge Dodgson and who was a close friend to Alice's family. One of the photographs showed Alice when she was seven years old. Benjamin said she immediately started thinking, "Hmmm... I wonder what ever happened to her?" This is how she started writing her book *Alice I Have Been* and re-introduced the world to Alice both as a book character and a real person.

I think about this story every time I get a chance to "change the scenery". Indeed, last year, for two months, I had to go to the city three or four times a week. During that period of time, new ideas and insights simply kept FLOODING into my head, so much so that I had to quickly capture them in my journal before they disappeared. It is not only the new things I saw, but also the new perspectives from which I got to see everything that was ever familiar to me. I remember walking along the streets like a tourist, oohing and aahing all the time, looking at here and there with a brand new sense of wonder and awe. The world moved on, people moved on, but I could stand there, forever, just like a statue who can see into eternity.

The other day I went to the city, and the same thing happened again. I was reading Stephen King's novel *Mr Mercedes* and suddenly an idea came into my head. Just as I was busy recording it in my journal, the man sitting next to me started chatting with two tourists who were on their way to a famous scenic spot in Melbourne. The man was really friendly, recommending plenty of excellent things to see and do around the city. As I heard their laughing, excited voices, I could not help but think – yeah, right, here I was, sitting calmly and plotting a fictional story of cold murder and psychological thrill. It was hilarious!

What was the last place you travelled to? Do you think one day you would like to travel to Australia and even Melbourne? I would love to hear from you.

Yours Sincerely,
Christine

#14: Book Giving

February 14, 2015
To: C.S., Brownsboro, Alabama, U.S.A.

Dear C,

Greetings from Australia. Today is Valentine's Day! More importantly, it is the International Book Giving Day! Do you like reading? Do you read much? Who are your favourite authors, and what kind of books do you enjoy reading?

It is only mid-February, and I have already bought five books from one of the online retailers here in Australia. I can only afford to buy books when they are on sale, so these are good bargains. I keep a list of interesting titles, so I can always find something to buy whenever there is a sale.

While online retailers are often blamed for the demise of independent bookstores, I think otherwise, because they do make it extremely convenient for readers like me, with no easy access to brick-and-mortar stores, to buy books. A couple of clicks on screen and three to five days of waiting, and *viola!* The doorbell rings and my books have arrived. How delightful!

Mind you, I do support the one and only real bookstore in our community, whenever I can get there. The fact that I need to point this out shows how politically correct it is to show such support. These days people would eye you differently if you openly declare how much you enjoy buying and reading ebooks. Different from using iPhone, iPad and "smart" things like that, which are considered to be cool and classy, buying and reading ebooks from online retailers is often seen as a "betrayal" of "real" literature and reading. (Interestingly, buying print books from online retailers is still acceptable, although we are often urged to support home-grown businesses instead of international giants such as the dreaded Amazon.com.)

The same applies to self-publishing. Writers who take full control of their publishing journeys still have to deal with the common misconception that they are not as good as their traditionally published peers in terms of quality and prestige. A perfect example is how reluctant many writers are when facing offers from ebook publishers and self-publishing services. Although these writers desperately want to be known and loved by readers out there, they would rather wait to be picked up by a traditional publisher, something that rarely happens. It is either traditional publishing or nothing at all.

These days, I guess, even self-published and ebook writers secretly aspire to win the affection (and affirmation) of traditional publishers. It is almost like self-publishing and ebooks are in their eyes merely "stepping stones" to "real" success. In the same way that love on Valentine's Day is commonly expressed with roses and boxes of chocolate, these writers need something concrete in their hands. They can only feel successful (and secure) when holding their own title as a print book with a traditional publisher's logo on the cover.

Do I sound like an old grumpy gal? You bet! An avid reader who also writes and publishes, I have seen many excellent writings buried deep in the dark and secret drawers of their writers or in the even darker and more secret databases of their literary agents. These writers and agents are waiting for a chance to connect with traditional publishers. They have waited, are still waiting, and will continue to wait for an opportunity that may never come, because traditional publishers seldom look back at old writings. Neither do they pay much attention to non-bestselling and non-award winning titles.

So there are plenty of writers and agents who would rather wait patiently in the dark for a highly unlikely chance to shine. Very often it is such a long wait that they have gone stale. Perfect bottles of wine have turned into vinegar. Men and women who were once young, energetic and ambitious are now old, bitter and cynical. Dreams have turned into delusions, then deliriums, then descriptions in one of literary history's numerous forgotten pages. As time goes by, even these will become smudged and then whited out to make room for newly published titles.

Are you a writer as well? Do you know someone who writes and wants to get published? On this International Book Giving Day, I feel like asking all the writers out there to give themselves a book. Publish your writings in every format and through every channel there is under the sun, so that they can exist as books and be *remembered*. So that they can be *read*. In the same way that information will never automatically turn into knowledge or even wisdom, a valuable piece of writing will remain a pile of paper if it is not published. Give yourself a book that is your own writing – that is the best Valentine's Day gift you can find.

Yours Sincerely,
Christine

On Life, Love, Literature & Letter Writing

#15: Being a Migrant

February 15, 2015
To: B.F., Belfast, Northern Ireland, U.K.

Dear B,

Greetings from Australia. Today, February 15, marks the 18th anniversary of my arrival in Australia. I am a proud Aussie now, but there are still many things about this brilliant multicultural society that I need to learn and understand.

I often feel that it is more than citizenship that makes us belong to a country. Indeed, how do we claim a country as our own? How do we identify with it? If we were not part of its collective past, then can we possibly contribute to the making of its collective future? Of course we can. When I came to Australia, I very much wanted it to be my home, where my loved ones live, where my career thrives, where my roots are. After all these years, I reckon I have done OK in these aspects.

I have spent years studying the nature and significance of identity. To me, identity concerns not only how one perceives oneself but also how one is received by others. When we talk about identity, we cannot ignore either aspect.

To me, identity is a curious thing, because it is flexible in nature but has profound impact on how people associate with each other. At any one moment we can have a dozen different identities, given by both the others and ourselves, which affect how we behave with individuals and groups. As that moment passes on to the next, our identities also change, with our thoughts and deeds altering accordingly. For example, I speak and act in considerably different ways as a mother, a wife, a writer, a translator, a journalist, and an independent scholar. People's views and expectations about me also change dramatically as they identify me in any one of these six ways.

Thus we have stereotypes, which can be both positive and negative, depending on the political, economic, social and cultural circumstances under which we live. Stereotypes are constructed to help us understand something unknown. Once we have understood it, our views may or may not change, again depending on our personal circumstances. This is not the point. THE POINT IS we need to understand stereotypes are not "standards" or "norms". Neither are they "natural". We cannot rely on stereotypes to form our views, without firstly reflecting for a moment whether these man-made categories can truly help us appreciate the values of the others.

These days I have learned there is no use complaining what stereotypes other people may have about us. Instead, we should do something to change people's prejudices. Throughout the past 18 years I have worked really hard to understand Australia's historical and cultural characteristics, to participate in a wide range of social and literary activities, and to behave in the "Australian way". Indeed, the consensus here is that to be an Australian is to respect and uphold a sense of a "fair go", to appreciate the differences between all individuals and groups and treat them all equally, in order to sustain a truly multicultural society.

I love this view. I believe that when we make the decision to migrate to a new country, we do not just go there to enjoy all the benefits it can give us. Instead, we need to do our best to belong to that country, to give back what we can, in order to enrich its society and culture. To be a migrant in today's much globalised world is *not* to expect an automatic acceptance and trust by the others. Instead, we have to work hard to *earn* it. The foundational principles of multiculturalism such as mutual respect and tolerance cannot and should not be used as an excuse to ignore what unites the whole country – the one voice that affirms and speaks for that country's social and cultural values. Being a migrant is to give, not just to receive. We cannot simply pursue our dreams without caring for the ground on which we stand and live.

Well, that is enough rambling already. Part of this derives from feelings about this unusual day in my personal history, but it also reminds me of the fact that you are based in Belfast. Talk about stereotypes! I would love to hear your views on issues such as national and personal identities.

Yours Sincerely,
Christine

On Life, Love, Literature & Letter Writing

#16: Searching for the Past

February 16, 2015
To: K.H., Seoul, South Korea

Dear K,

Greetings from Australia. How is everything in South Korea? I saw your self-introduction as an expatriate American there who does not speak or read the Korean language. Life must be a bit tough for you. Do you miss home?

These days the concept of "home" is not necessarily a real location. To me, it is more like a moment in time. It was a time when I became aware of who I was and what I wanted to do for life. It was a time of reaching maturity in more ways than merely physically, of being sensitive to other people's views and ideologies while trying desperately to establish some of my own. It was a time of experiencing not only the bright and sweet aspects of life but also those that were dark, bitter, unforgivable and unforgettable. It was a time of saying hello, but also one of waving goodbye.

I once heard an elderly writer talking about his idea of "home". He said when one leaves home – in this sense not only one's hometown but one's homeland as well – everything about that place becomes frozen in one's memory. All one remembers is that place in that particular moment in time. Despite the fact that life goes on and "the only thing constant is change" (quoted from *Jekyll & Hyde* the musical), only that specific memory serves as a caricature of "home", a psychological landmark that one uses to position oneself throughout life's journey. This is why when one eventually gets to go home, it feels so close yet so far away – as time goes by, home has become such a brand new place that it feels almost like a different country. Eventually one would rather remain in one's adopted country forever, because it is the only place with which one feels familiar and to which one belongs.

Indeed, how can one belong to a memory, a distant dream, something that is forever lost in reality? One can go searching for the past, like Richard Collier's search for Elise McKenna in Richard Matheson's famous science fiction novel *Bid Time Return* (later made into the even more famous movie *Somewhere in Time*, starring Christopher Reeve and Jane Seymour). But such a search would only be futile.

This afternoon I was browsing the Internet, and was surprised to find a video of a "flash mob" event in suburban Taipei, Taiwan – where I was born and raised. You may have heard of this term before – according to Wikipedia, a "flash mob" is "a group of people who assemble suddenly in a public place, perform an unusual and seemingly pointless act for a brief time, before quickly dispersing. They are often used for the purpose of entertainment, satire or artistic expression and are organised via telecommunications, social media, or viral emails".

I should mention here that the first video of a "flash mob" event I saw online is that of a group of local residents from a town called Tecoma, near where I live. In the video, they burst into the foot court of a shopping mall and started singing "Do You Hear the People Sing?" from *Les Miserables* the musical (and later the movie, starring Hugh

Jackman and Russell Crowe and Anna Hathaway), in protest of McDonald's push to set up a branch there, right across the street from a primary school and forcing a lot of local shops to either shut down or relocate. The local government decided not to grant a building permit to McDonald's, but it was overruled by the state govenrment. Nonetheless, the video touched a lot of people's hearts and contributed to a successful crowd-sourcing campaign online to raise money for the town's representatives to fly from Australia to Chicago to negotiate with McDonald's headquarters. (Sadly, the eating outlet was still built.)

Well, in the video I saw today, the flash mob was a group of more than 100 volunteers who burst into a train station in suburban Taipei to perform a series of "campus folk songs" that have been popular in Taiwan since the mid-1970s. These songs are like those by Bob Dylan and Joan Baez in the United States or those by the Beatles in the United Kingdom. They are absolutely well-known to many, many people as the latter left their teenage years behind to march into their 20s and even 30s. These are songs, in short, of innocence. The sort of courageous but naive youth that existed in everyone's past and that everyone looked back to from time to time with a sigh. They are the dreams lost.

So I sat there and watched the video... and burst into tears after only 10 seconds. I cried, quietly, throughout the whole five-minute show... Then I mopped off my tears and went on with my life.

But my heart ached... and I cannot find a proper English word to describe how I feel. "Homesickness" is too plain, too childish and absolutely negative ("sickness", ugh!). "Nostalgia" is too mild and too poetic to convey that straightforward, fierce sense of sorrowful but futile remembering. "Yearning" will do but always reminds me of the word "yawn". As for "longing"... well, there is no use longing for anything when you know you have to leave it behind, because it *hurts* when you look back.

Now, as I write to you, I am back to my normal self. "Home is where the heart is" and my heart has been here in Australia for the past 18 years. Still, it helps for one to pour everything out from time to time, I guess, so one can be empty enough to be again filled up with life's new adventures. Are you having a series of adventures there, as well? Do you plan to go home eventually or set up a new life and career in South Korea? I would love to hear your story.

Yours Sincerely,
Christine

#17: Law and Literature

February 17, 2015
To: K.R., Dunellen, New Jersey, U.S.A.

Dear K,

Greetings from Australia. Thank you for sending your first InCoWriMo letter to me. It is a delightful surprise to find it in my mailbox. How is everything going in New Jersey?

Glad to meet one more professional in the legal field. Even more glad to know that you also read and write on the train. To me, travelling by train is a luxury and a good opportunity to observe what other people are reading. What triggers people to start reading a particular book? Do they enjoy it? Or are they just killing time? I find it hard *not* to start a conversation on anything and everything about reading, especially when I see people reading a book that I love! Which is why it is really annoying when someone is reading from his or her mobile phone or tablet, as I have no idea what the content is about!

Writing on the train makes my already-messy handwriting even worse. However, I find it really inspiring to observe the scenery both outside and within the carriage – the landscape, traffic, technology and people and how they interact with and impact on each other. I have learned to carry a journal and record all the new and crazy ideas looming in my head. While some of them remain as buds that are yet to blossom, others have been tweaked this way and that to become either short stories or private jokes that make me smile all the way to my destination. People probably think me weird!

And what makes lawyers great writers? You mentioned you already have a novel – what is it about? I am lucky to have some really good working relationships with various lawyers who are published authors. They are invariably very straightforward and friendly, and meticulously patient when discussing the rights and obligations specified in their publishing contracts with me. As I translate their writings into Chinese, I see – and more often *feel* – their existence between the lines as individuals who are passionate about life. It is not so much right and wrong they care about, but what causes people to draw the line between them. I find this immensely fascinating, to be able to get a glimpse of the workings of an intelligent brain.

Is it because lawyers are often the pioneers into the wildness that is people's mind? The bright and dark sides of the moon, the known and unknown and the twilight zone in-between. Is it because people more or less have to trust their lawyers in order to win their lawsuits? Does the law always help to uncover the truth, the whole truth and nothing but the truth? Or, perhaps we have been under too much influence by famous authors such as John Grisham to really understand the nature and significance of law. The stereotypes, biases, prejudices and myths about lawyers – to what extent have they not only enriched but also damaged the legal profession as a literary subject?

Perhaps in your next train journey you would like to tell me what you think. Consider it as a response to a kid's question of what you do and why you like writing. It is my belief that to be able to write, you must have a unique voice and want to have it heard. Because of this, we are all writers as we enjoy and record the grand train journey that is life.

    Please take care. I look forward to hearing from you.

Yours Sincerely,
Christine

#18: Life Writing & Sharing

February 18, 2015
To: B.C., Huntsville, Alabama, U.S.A.

Dear B,

Greetings from Australia. I was both surprised and delighted to find your letter because it was C who had promised to write. It is wonderful to know that you both are passionate about letter writing and blogging. This convinces me that you must be sharing a love for reading, too. I think it is one of the best things a man and his wife can do.

This is the first year I participate in InCoWriMo. I have to admit it is hard – so much of my time is spent on other people's writings that I rarely have time to do any of my own. (As a translator and publisher of Chinese ebooks, I help Chinese and English authors worldwide to promote their writings to the Chinese world.) Still, my resolution this year is to write and publish more – blogging, journaling, participating in InCoWriMo and even NaPoWriMo, and joining book clubs and literary festivals. Who knows? Perhaps I will even try self-publishing.

I have a naive fascination about the Vietnam War. Any war, really. I believe each nation has at least one key event that helps to determine its role, not only what it does on the international stage, but also how its people think and feel about it in history. In Australia such an event is often perceived to be the Battle of Gallipoli in 1915-1916, where 8,709 Australian soldiers died and more than 19,440 injured.

Considering the fact that Australia's population at the time was less than five million, it means every town big and small had lost some young men at the campaign; and even in those cases where they were lucky to have come back, their lives were forever changed, often towards the bitter side. Even today there are plenty of Australians wondering why such a miserable defeat helped to forge us as a nation, creating an "Australianness" that is unique from its status as a member of the Commonwealth. As a migrant, I find this kind of soul-searching absolutely inspiring.

Ultimately, I think, it is all about life. We record our stories to share the past, and to learn from it so that we will have a future. I am interested in reading (and hopefully writing) stories of extraordinary individuals through turbulent times such as natural and man-made disasters. Yet it is unfortunate that people have to pay such a dramatic and traumatic price as war to learn to grow up.

From war to photography, which is also a sharing of life, the happy and bright side of humanity, the forever young part of us, moments to be celebrated and cherished. Knowing nothing about photography – and any sort of visual art, really – I have long learned to transform images into words. Indeed, I can only draw square cows, but in writing my cows can FLY.

You mentioned Neville Shute and how you fell in love with Australia via his books. Well, I only knew his *A Town Like Alice* and *On the Beach* – both are very sad yet beautiful, and I love them for their revelation of hope among the ruined people and landscape. What is your favourite book by him?

I hope that one day you and C will have time to visit Australia.

When you do, feel free to let me know so we can have a cuppa together. I love this country, where I can just be ME and no one else. It is a different sort of freedom from that in the United States, I think. Occasionally unsophisticated but very often so straightforward that all you can do is to laugh your heart out. We are a people of sunlight, and we love to share our joy.

Keep writing. I look forward to hearing from you and C.

Yours Sincerely,
Christine

#19: Modern-Day Letter Writing

February 19, 2015
To: N.T., Tokyo, Japan

Dear N,

Greetings from Australia. Happy Chinese New Year! Do you know any Chinese individual or group who celebrates this traditional festival? It certainly looks very interesting on television.

Originally from Taiwan, I am ethnically and culturally Chinese. However, I have not been celebrating Chinese festivals and traditional events throughout my years in Australia – life goes on and there is no time to relax. I suppose I do cherish my Chineseness, but it is not something I can or need to show people by doing things with specific Chinese characteristics. I do not need to act like a Chinese to prove that I am one. Besides, exactly what kind of cultural traits does one need to display in order to be recognised as a Chinese?

Traditionally, Chinese people believe every kitchen has a god who oversees the performance of the household throughout the year. On New Year's Day, he is supposed to return to Heaven to deliver a report, so the Jade Emperor can decide how to reward the household with blessings for the coming year. Because of this, people always cook lots of sweet dishes on New Year's Eve as offerings (read: bribes) to the Kitchen God, so that he will speak sweetly for the family.

Well, these days governments and all kinds of multicultural businesses monitor our daily activities through our use of the Internet, so if the Kitchen God does exist, he will definitely lose his job as a result of fierce competition. I have learned not to write anything that really matters on any computer connecting to the Web. Perhaps this is also the reason why people never give up writing letters. Today, the good old-fashioned snail mail is probably the safest way to transmit a message. We value our privacy so much that we are willing to wait for something to be delivered from Point A to Point B. Patience is now truly a virtue – and necessity – something that we are increasingly losing in this day and age of the Internet.

What an interesting world we live in now. As we move forward, the past takes on new meanings that are potentially capable of transforming our lives. The other day I saw a news item regarding a proposal by the Japanese Post to purchase a prominent freight company here in Australia. As letter writing becomes increasingly rare, but with delivery of packages and parcels booming as a result of increasing online shopping, the aforementioned company appears to have a bright future. Will the commonly perceived diligence and efficiency of the Japanese people further enhance the Australian company's performance and benefit all who still rely on snail mail? We shall wait and see.

Indeed, we live in a very interesting world. What is your view about letter writing? How is it going in Japan? I would love to hear about it from you.

Yours Sincerely,

Christine

On Life, Love, Literature & Letter Writing

#20: Reading Friends from Afar

February 20, 2015
To: V.B., Medford, Massachusetts, U.S.A.

Dear V,

Greetings from Australia. Many thanks for your beautiful letter, which I received yesterday. I love the envelope's design and the saying, "The dream has grown up a size larger than before." It makes me think of a baby's smile.

I love stationary, too, although I appreciate paper more than pens. (I am sure I will write more if my handwriting can be as nice as yours.) Piles of blank paper always give me joy and hope – all the stories I could possibly write on them! While I have been writing with computers since my teenage days, I am sure I will get to do some creative writing on paper one day.

Japan is indeed an amazing country in terms of stationary. I was in Tokyo once and visited a shop specialising in paper – all five storeys of it, from notebooks to letter pads to sketching and wrapping paper and calendars of all shapes and sizes. It was like a paradise! Which is why I admire the Japanese – as a people they love and excel in art. Pens intimidate me, but paper helps me dream.

Here in Australia we started to have some very nice paper in recent years. Not necessarily for writing, I am afraid, but to use it for wrapping brings great happiness to people's lives. I believe a nicely decorated present itself is a symbol of love. It is like a special font that is both practical and artistic, especially when it is printed on paper.

You asked what it is like to live "on the opposite side of the world". It is an interesting concept, as we all perceive the world from our own perspectives, using our own yardsticks to measure those outside and beyond our known boundaries. One of my friends has a brother who has designed a map showing the whole world upside-down. In this case, North America and Europe are the "peripheries" while Australia and our brother New Zealand are like the Middle Earth in J.R.R. Tolkien's *The Lord of the Rings*, where Mr Bilbo Baggins proudly announces while "smoking and blowing smoke-rings":

"[In these parts] We are plain quiet folk and have no use for adventures. Nasty disturbing uncomfortable things! Make you late for dinner! I can't think what anybody sees in them!"

Well, we Australians love adventures (as we know Bilbo does), but we love having a stable and comfortable life even more. It is like having a good rest after a day's hard work, sitting at home where we have everything except worries and concerns of money and security. Australians are not ambitious in terms of wealth and fame. Which is probably why we never had and most likely will never have a Great Gatsby. Australians are more like Babe the sheep pig and Mumble the Happy Feet. We are rich but humble in spirit. Everybody is a mate and deserves a fair go, and no one wants to be a tall poppy. We have sunlight and the Great Southern Ocean and plenty of smiles to share with the rest of the world.

I guess this is why Australians reach out – we dare to travel to all corners of the world because we know there is always a great life to come back to. We are very much like Sam who is willing to journey to

Mordor and confront the most fierce and evil enemy, but who is the happiest when he is back in the Shire with his girl and home cooking. That is the Aussie Spirit.

Australians love friends, and reading friends from afar are one of the things I consider to be the most precious. You asked whether I have read anything awesome recently. Mmmm, tough question. I love Stephen King's books and am currently reading *Mr Mercedes*, with *The Revival* being my next target. I am also reading Lisa Genova's *Still Alice*, a book I had always wanted to read since it was first published back in 2007. Like you, I find David Mitchell and Stieg Larsson interesting, thanks more to the movies adapted from their books than their actual writings, I am afraid. In this sense, I absolutely love *Life of Pi* – Yann Martel's story that is tremendously beautiful both as a book and a movie. I also admire Michael Ondaatje because of *The English Patient* – I love the movie and plan to read the book as well. I have heard his *Anil's Ghost* is a masterpiece, too.

I am more into popular fiction than literary writing. The books I never finished include Kazuo Ishiguro's *Never Let Me Go*, Kathryn Harrison's *The Seal Wife*, Audrey Niffenegger's *The Time Traveller's Wife* and Markus Zusak's *The Book Thief*, just to name a few. Yet, I can sit there for hours re-reading The Hunger Games, the Twilight Saga, the Harry Potter books and obviously all of Stephen King's titles. Strangely, one of the "serious" authors I absolutely adore is Justin Cronin – I have loved *The Passage* and *The Twelve* and am now eagerly waiting for *The City of Mirrors*. Can Alice Sebold be considered a "serious" author as well? If yes, then I admit I cried like a baby over *Lovely Bones* and will be happy to shed more tears over *The Almost Moon*.

I should be reading more, much more. You mentioned Haruki Murakami's *The Strange Library* and I am keen to check it out. In your next letter, please feel free to tell me more about the great books you have read. I love hearing from good friends *and* about reading good books.

Yours Sincerely,
Christine

#21: Life in Other Lands

February 21, 2015
To: G.A., Hopkinton, Massachusetts, U.S.A.

Dear G,

Greetings from Australia. Thank you very much for the lovely postcard, and for sending it to me while you were travelling through the famous Yosemite National Park. I was there once, very briefly, to admire that ancient Half Dome from the distance, which resembles a face staring into eternity. I read online that in one native American legend it is the face of a mother, while in another it is that of a young girl. Either way, it is a tear-stricken face, behind which many sad stories may be hidden. I am sure it has inspired numerous writers and poets to explore the universal themes of unfulfillment, loss and regret.

You mentioned you recently moved from Canada to the United States. May I ask why? Are you by yourself or with family? I studied in Ohio for two years, for a degree in journalism. Before and after that, I also visited different parts of America, for various reasons and lengths of time. In my mind, it is always a great country – so vibrant and confident, so full of youthful ideals.

If Australia used to be a nation riding the sheep's back (i.e. for a whole century, until the 1990s at least, the wool industry gave Australia one of the highest living standards in the world), then the United States has always been a country built on dreams. Dreamers go there and become successful if they are lucky. Otherwise, they wither and die dreaming. To me, Americans remain young at heart because they are and will always be dreamers. It does not sustain them as a superpower forever, but other rising giants, especially China, will find it hard to catch up to the United States without a similar belief in, pursuit for and protection of innovation.

On the other hand, Australia, perhaps like Canada, has no desire to be a superpower. I have studied and translated various Canadian authors and watched enough children's television programs produced there to know that it is a great country. After all, Australia learned its multiculturalism policies from Canada. Australia takes pride of its society as a salad bowl, where all kinds of fruit co-exist to help creating a wonderful flavour of harmony. I am sure people of Canada feel the same. We encourage integration, instead of assimilation. We are not a pot in which all differences are to be melted.

I am an ethnic Chinese from Taiwan. While both China and Taiwan are monocultural societies, in recent years the concept of globalisation and multiculturalism have reached that part of the world and are slowly impacting its mainstream and multiple sub-cultures in a positive way. Still, there is a lot of room for improvement, particularly in overseas Chinese communities. Indeed, in Australia, the only racial discrimination I have ever witnessed throughout my 18 years here was in my alma mater. A Chinese colleague and I were discussing something with an Australian lecturer who is also a white person. As soon as our Aussie friend left, the Chinese colleague switched to Mandarin and said to me: "Let's not be bothered with the foreigner and do things our way." I was flabbergasted. I could never forget that sneer on his face. It serves as my constant reminder that a smile and an open mind make a huge difference when you live in someone else's country. You can make it your home and be content, or you can forever consider the locals as "foreign devils" and live like an alien.

Life in other lands can be easy or hard. To me, it all depends on how much we want to embrace that land and the people living there. For however long you intend to stay in the Untied States, I wish you a happy and free life like a fish in water. It is how I feel here in Australia.

Yours Sincerely,
Christine

#22: One Letter at a Time

February 22, 2015
To: D.H.H., Hanoi, Vietnam

Dear D,

Greetings from Australia. Glad to have met you via InCoWriMo 2015. At first, what attracted my attention was your "1000 Letters" project. Then a search online led me to your website and various social media pages where samples of your calligraphy are displayed. What beautiful writing you have there!

You mentioned that you have been studying calligraphy and penmanship since you were a little boy, and that your grandfather and father were both calligraphers with great achievements, which inspired you into studying this art. How interesting it is that our family plays a crucial role in shaping our lives. Whether or not they have specifically told us to choose one career over another, or to marry this person instead of that one – deep in our hearts we feel their positive and/or negative impact on us, which serves as a contributing factor to the making of our decisions in such a fundamental way that very often we are simply unaware of it. Our ancestors are part of us, in our blood, bones and genes, dreams, and memories. Through us, they live forever. It remains my hope that my art, too, can live forever through my children.

I was lucky to have my wedding invitation designed by a renowned calligrapher here in Australia. His name is Rodney Saulwick.

In 1982, he was commissioned to produce a calligraphic presentation to Queen Elizabeth in commemoration of her opening of Australia's National Gallery. Rodney was actually my husband's friend and colleague, but from him I have learned so much about being sincere with life and your art. He and his wife later attended our wedding and danced as gracefully as it is ever possible for two naughty kids to do so. Both of them were very old, with lots of silver hair and constant bursts of hearty laughter. I often think that throughout that party, the most brilliant couple was them. It was the same when we attended his funeral several months later – a jolly event celebrating his life's achievements and all those amazing memories people have about him. We all danced along some crazy Russian folk music, going around in circles and kicking our legs high. He would have approved of that wild party if he had been there – and I believe he was.

(Note: You can still see some of Rodney Saulwick's calligraphic work online at: http://www.saulwickartonline.com/misc/sad.html, under "calligraphy".)

Indeed, I am sure that you, too, have learned the lesson of being sincere with yourself and the world from Ms Margaret Shepherd. I imagine doing calligraphy is like writing – you do it one letter at a time, pouring all your heart and soul into it and making it a living art. I imagine it is like your 1000 letters – you work so hard to earn enough money to buy those envelopes and stamps and send your good wishes to all corners of the world. Friends and strangers alike are granted with a piece of your art, which brings joy and makes their lives a little more pleasant. That is what artists do.

Are there a lot of people writing letters to you? Seeing their handwriting is like meeting them in person, as you, among all, would know how a person's inner beauty is revealed through his or her hand. Perhaps you can clearly read them in this way, like Sherlock Holmes, the legendary detective who is capable of seeing the whole world within a grain of sand. Indeed, Holmes can be a great poet if he is ever bothered to use pen and paper.

As for us, who refer to ourselves as artists, our job is to describe this world in as many splendid ways as possible, to present its beauty and joy to the next generation and the one after that, in the same way that your ancestors had done it for you. In that small part of the world you are creating life that will hopefully never be shadowed again by conflicts and chaos. You have to believe in that.

May I take this chance to wish you all the best with your fundraising project. I hope you get to live your dream, to mingle with people like you and learn from each other, to experience different cultures while sharing your own, and to make this world a little bit better through your calligraphy like all artists do.

Yours Sincerely,

Christine

#23: Letter-Writing "Celebrities"?

February 23, 2015
To: N.F., Seattle, Washington, U.S.A.

Dear N,

Greetings from Australia. Thank you for sharing on the InCoWriMo website, various titles on the art and craft of letter writing. I checked them out on Amazon.com and realised they are more related to the actual act of writing various types of letters. I also found a whole bunch of interesting books and articles on the history and cultural significance of letter writing, including British journalist and author Simon Garfield's *To the Letter: A Celebration of the Lost Art of Letter Writing*. You might want to take a look at this book, too.

I find it interesting that in recent years, a series of famous media outlets – from *The Guardian* and *The New Yorker* to *Wall Street Journal* and *Huffington Post* – have started exploring the LOST art of letter writing. Here in Australia, as InCoWriMo took off, this art – whether it is lost or not – also became a focus of public interest, at least in the literary arena. Indeed, one of Melbourne's leading literary organisations sponsored a workshop on letter writing. The presenter is an author and journalist who also co-curates a bestselling Australian literary salon called Women of Letters.

I am interested in letter writing because I love writing and sharing. While the former may be a private act, the latter is certainly social in nature. With that said, I did not get to attend the aforementioned workshop – too expensive for non-members. But I did check out everything about it online. The presenter enlightened her audience on a diverse range of issues, from the history of letter writing to why the act now enjoys a revival. More importantly, she explored "what sets performative letters apart from other storytelling methods; how to write and craft a letter to be shared in public; and how to successfully navigate the private and the public elements of letter writing".

I find these issues interesting because, to me, InCoWriMo is only partly about the conduct of private and ongoing conversations between families and friends. A more prominent part of this movement is to make new friends and discover new grounds – "to explore strange new worlds, to seek out new life and new civilisations, to boldly go where no (wo)man has gone before" (see *Star Trek*). By actively sending out letters to unknown people in unknown places, we hope to broaden our horizons. We want to have our voices heard by others and hear back from them.

Note this order – to shout out and then to hear a response, or at least an echo. We cannot sit at home and hope for letters to drop in, perhaps as automatically *and magically* as those soaring into Harry Potter's house on the eve of his eleventh birthday. Instead, we need to ask. We need to *act*.

Somehow I cannot help but wonder: If what we want is to cross boundaries, both intellectually and emotionally, then are our letters communicative or performative? A bit of both, I think. In our letters we want to be informative and entertaining. We want to be both creative and impressive, to attract people's attention so that they will respond.

Perhaps letter writing these days has become a part of what we know as social media, delivered via snail mail instead of the Internet. Look at the amount of information exchanged on the InCoWriMo website – "I have sent you a letter and hope you would write back" and "Please write to me and I will definitely respond". In this sense, what makes letter writing different from using Facebook and Twitter?

The aforementioned literary salon Women of Letters also sounds interesting. According to Wikipedia, a salon is "a gathering of people under the roof of an inspiring host, held partly to amuse one another and partly to refine the taste and increase the knowledge of the participants through conversation". More importantly, these gatherings "often consciously follow (Roman lyric poet) Horace's definition of the aims of poetry, 'either to please or to educate'". In other words, to be both entertaining and informative, which is what we want for letter writing.

Indeed, according to the website of Women of Letters, it is "an afternoon that celebrates a diverse range of strong female talent whilst simultaneously raising funds for [a charity organisation]... The monthly occasion brings together [the] best and brightest writers, musicians, politicians and comedians in celebration of the beautiful lost art of letter writing". Surely these celebrities are both informative and entertaining? Indeed, in March, two events are to take place in New York City in the Northern Hemisphere and Melbourne here in Australia. The ladies to be featured in the NYC event are a "revered film and stage actor and director", an "iconic actress and (movie) star", an "award-winning and *New York Times* bestselling author", a "beloved pond-hopping writer and comedian", a "sartorial icon and fashion designer", and a "critically-acclaimed stand-up comic and writer". All proceeds will go to the New York Women's Foundation.

While reading this, a series of images surfaced in the dark pool that is my mind, like those in *My Fair Lady*: Ladies dressed in white milling around a meticulously manicured lawn, wearing white gloves and hats decorated with colourful ribbons, their cheeks rosy and lightly powdered, sipping champagne or white wine and dabbing their lips with white silky handkerchiefs, sampling tiny triangle sandwiches of thin slices of turkey and green cos lettuce leaves with a touch of cranberry dressing, carefully served by young girls in starched uniforms smiling politely. A silver bell chimed somewhere. All the ladies gathered in a large room with dark oak-panelled walls and a sparkling chandelier creating a friendly literary atmosphere. The ladies sat down and fanned themselves, ready to listen to high-class gossip and well-intentioned anecdotes on how their already sophisticated lifestyle might be further enhanced. They clapped politely, occasionally laughing softly, tapping on each other's shoulder to inquire quietly about the amount of donation attracted to the event. The afternoon passed leisurely. Then a short taxi ride took the ladies home where dinner was served by servants. Kids were well looked after. Husbands were again late, occupied by office business as usual. The ladies continued to chatter and babble until late into the night. Before going to bed, they left their pearl necklaces and ivory hairpins on the mantelpiece in the lounge room. Tomorrow would be another easy day.

Then a separate set of images emerged, like those in *Les Miserables*: Students and blue-collar workers gathered in a small pub on the street corner, their foreheads covered with sweat, their clothing stained by dirt, grass, diesel and metal grease, their sleeves rolled up, showing muscles, some with tattoos on their arms. Drinking pints of beer and eating plain bread rolls and watery porridge, cursing at each other's good or bad daily fortunes, teasing the shy but beautiful maids and the cook's focus on quantity instead of quality, roaring with laughter. After the meal they quieted down, listening intensively to an awkward poem or a piece of prose fiction shared by some self-styled writer, mocking at their raw but passionate voice, arguing loudly whether it had any practical meaning or value. Then the discussion turned into debates on liberty, equality and fraternity. Topics and beer flowed freely. No one was polite. Indeed the conversations were quite rude, but everybody was happy in a drowsy way. Late into the night they parted company, singing loudly and slapping on each other's back as they stumbled home to have a quick sleep before getting up early the next morning to go to work. There was no extra energy for dreaming. Dreams were for rich people in the upper class.

 I shook my head. Do all of these imagined scenes matter? Not really. Does letter writing have to be a purely intellectual, artistic, sophisticated and high-society activity, participated and enjoyed by people who have money, time and creative talents to spare? Not at all. We do not need to be celebrities to promote the writing of letters. We do not have to have a specific *purpose* to write, apart from sharing our daily thoughts and feelings. We do not have to be highly civilised in our writing – gossiping will do, too, as long as it makes us think and laugh in the process. Why, we do not even need to think. We just *feel* – feeling the power of words, feeling loved by families and friends, feeling accepted by someone out there in the distance. Letter writing creates a sense of togetherness. The time and effort it takes to write a letter, send it out and wait for a response helps to fulfil our soul. We are not alone.

So that is enough sharing from me... I look forward to hearing what you think of the books on letter writing as an art, whether it is indeed lost or not. Who have you been writing to, so far?

Yours Sincerely,
Christine

On Life, Love, Literature & Letter Writing

#24: Dealing with Rejections

February 24, 2015
To: S.S., Quebec City, Quebec, Canada

Dear S,

Greetings from Australia. I saw on the InCoWriMo website that you would like to receive some letters. As a journalist, your life must be very busy and exciting. I hope this letter from the other side of the world can bring you some extra joy.

You must have been through a lot to reach your current position. Did you always want to be a journalist, or is this something that just happened? "Nothing *just happens!*" I imagine you would say. Indeed, I have learned that our life is very much a result of all the decisions we have made -- there is hardly anything that is coincidental. Still, because it is extremely difficult to foresee what will happen when we make a decision, we can only do our best and be prepared to face the consequences.

I used to have plenty of what I perceived to be very good ideas. When I thought of something I often did it straight away, and braced myself for whatever consequences there might be much later. Throughout the years, however, I have learned to avoid making quick and uneducated decisions. I have also learned to better prepare myself for the results, especially the emotional impact they may have on me.

Take today, one that has been full of ups and downs. In the morning, I received an email notification that my application for a voluntary position was rejected. I had perceived myself to be one of the very few people who are qualified for this job, but obviously I was wrong. Worse, because I had very strong (and arrogant?) views on how the tasks involved could be completed, I had made the mistake of undermining the employer's specific expectations. My interview with them practically ruined my chance of being appointed for this position.

After that notification, another email informed me that a short story I recently submitted to an online literary magazine was rejected. Reason: It was not what they wanted. Oh, what a day! Two rejections in a row! Fuming, I turned off the computer and went to wash dishes in the kitchen. It was lucky that I did not break anything.

In the afternoon I returned to my computer... and was surprised to find a third email telling me that I had been selected as part of an "audience advocate group" for a major literary event here in Melbourne, Australia. I was speechless! They only chose twelve out of a total of 280 applicants, and I was one of them! Wow!

Now that I am writing to you, late at night, I reflect on what happened today. Among my many shortcomings, I find the hardest to admit is that I might not be as talented as I have previously thought. Or, I should say, having talents is one thing, but knowing how to fully and appropriately utilise them is another. Even more difficult is to accept rejections and criticism and transform them into a positive force that propels us to move on and make improvements.

So I have decided to contribute as much as I can to this forthcoming literary event as a volunteer. Meanwhile, I wrote to the aforementioned organisation that rejected me, thanked them for the interview, and asked for feedback so that I could learn to improve myself. Finally, I started working on a book of short stories, beginning with that little one that was rejected by the online magazine. While a window was shut on me, it has led me to discover a series of doors that may open if I well prepare myself to knock on them.

Well, it has been an unusual day for me... Do you have any special story of being rejected that later led to your success? I look forward to hearing from you.

Yours Sincerely,

Christine

On Life, Love, Literature & Letter Writing

#25: Hands in Friendship

February 25, 2015
To: P.L., Delray Beach, Florida, U.S.A.

Dear P,

Greetings from Australia. Thank you very much for sending me a "hand in friendship". What a graceful shape your hand has!

You said you had a peek at my website. Well, guess what? I also had a good look at yours. All those hands from all over the world – they are wonderful testimonies of what we want for and from this world, i.e. friendship, kindness, love, memory, and joy. An open hand is a gesture of peace. A wave, a hello, a sincere greeting – a step closer to what we Chinese refer to as the "Great Unity".

I wonder how you started your website? Such a dedicated collection of hands, with a such an impact on the people of the world. It reminds me, a lot, of the Pioneer Plaque and the Voyager Golden Record, which were sent to space by NASA in 1972 and 1977, respectively. But you are obviously doing much better than them – while they are still waiting for a response, you have had numerous friendly replies throughout the years!

I first started paying attention to hands in literature via Jeffery Deaver's *A Maiden's Grave*. In this brilliant novel, a deaf girl tricks a bunch of killers with sign language games to rescue a group of kidnapped students. Then it was *Red Dragon* by Thomas Harris, in which a blind girl gets the chance of a lifetime to touch a sleeping tiger.

She listens to its thundering heartbeat, sniffs at its mouth into which so much blood and flesh has gone and will continue to disappear, feels its warm breath on her face, and touches its lush fur that radiates both heat and power from its almighty body. It is a fascinating scene, with the act of touching by hand conveying so much desire to connect.

I also remember the little starfish-shaped hands of Hannibal Lecter's little sister Mischa in *Hannibal Rising*. Harris could have done a better job describing them and luring readers into that traumatised but mysterious mind that is Hannibal, but I guess he chose not to, for there is too much pain and sorrow in it.

A couple of years ago I read about a wonderful performance in the renowned Melbourne Writers Festival. It was a talk titled "Through Deaf Eyes", where a deaf author recited her story through sign language. The story was then interpreted by a "normal" person for the audience, who finally get a chance to comprehend what deaf people really think and feel. According to the author, Phoebe Tay, sign language is a spacial language that combines movements of hands and body and facial expressions. It also has its own grammar, punctuation and sentence structure and is therefore extremely difficult to convert to normal written English language. Most importantly, deaf authors are ultra-sensitive with the things they see. They pay attention to all forms of communication so that their narratives of emotions and events are often much more detailed and expressive. Whenever they use their hands, it is to convey not only words but also their innermost values. They lead us to a world that always exists but has been ignored by those who only listen and speak and even read with sounds.

Therefore, I think there is something extra precious about your "hands in friendship". It is a three-dimensional gesture of goodwill – people are willing to create a shape of their hands as an image, a photograph, a paper cut-out, etc, and send it to you via email or snail mail. It is almost like a signature, a personal promise that they are there and happy to reach out, a delivery of best wishes to both you and themselves, that everything is fine and will continue to be fine. A wave from a hand that is also an olive branch, fingers raised and splayed like the wings of a dove. A wave from the sea of people that rolls and rolls until it safely reaches a shore.

Well, I am going to send a hand to you, too. It will be my right hand, for I am right-handed. With that said, there is a famous poet in Taiwan who also writes excellent essays. He refers to the prose-oriented part of his personality as a "left-handed Muse", a term that has inspired thousands, if not tens of thousands, of writers across the Chinese World to explore the beauty of both poetry and prose.

I have recently started writing what people on Twitter refer to as "tiny little poems". In this sense, my "left-handed Muse" is trying very hard to understand what all the fuss is about with poetry. While this part of me walks (i.e. writes) in wobbly legs, trying to catch up to that part that is a little bit more experienced in composing prose and fiction, I am happy to also send an image of it to you. Two hands, double the friendship, all my best wishes.

Yours Sincerely,

Christine

On Life, Love, Literature & Letter Writing

#26: On Constructive Criticism

February 26, 2015
To: M.L., Brisbane, Queensland, Australia

Dear M,

Greetings from Melbourne. How is everything going in Brisbane? We have been communicating by email for more than a year now, but this time I want to write you a letter by hand via InCoWriMo (International Correspondence Writing Month).

You have always been very patient with me, particularly when I show a lack of progress. Your comments are always straightforward and positive, providing lots of constructive criticism to help me reflect on and learn from my mistakes. I have learned a lot from your professionalism. I am sure your clients bombard you with many more (un)reasonable requests than mine do me, but from the way you correspond with me, I know they are in the best hands there can ever be.

I used to dislike criticism. Really hated it. Criticism is a merciless needle whose job is to pop those balloons that are full of the hot air of self-deception. Worse, mixed in this air is often a fear disguised as self-confidence that is bordering arrogance. "Oh, how dare they, trying to interfere with the way I do things? This is my work and I'm the only one who knows how to do it." How familiar this sounds in my ears.

Only after I became a mother did I learn to face criticism. Kids are absolutely cruel when they eagerly provide what they think is the best advice for you. And there is nothing a mother can do about it, apart from trying (so very hard!) to comprehend that unkind but honest message and where its roots are. Once you sit down and think about it, you see the reasoning behind the unintended attack. You realise why it hurts so much, and it makes you want to shift the whole heaven and earth just to correct that tiny mistake in the eyes of your children.

So I learned to remain quiet whenever people criticise me, at least some of the time, I suppose. Although I still get angry, sad, annoyed and frustrated about it, I have learned to keep my mouth shut and force myself to think about those words that hurt me. I believe that most of the time people did not set out to attack me. The only reason why I feel hurt is because they have torn open something that I use to cover something I do not want the others to see – a wound, a weak spot, a mistake, a failure, or even a "dark side" of me that I cannot see. Worse, it may be something that I have long refused to see, like an ingrown toenail. Then it would be a typical case of cutting open the wound to help it heal.

Well, occasionally, people do try to hurt me. There is a poison in their words and a hint of malicious sneer in the way they are written, although I never know who the writers really are in cyberspace. When this happens – which is rather rare – no response is the best response. I turn myself into a piece of blank paper. Those who want news, good or bad, can go straight to the news agency.

Which is why your constructive criticism is so precious, not only to me but also to all those you communicate to and with. To me, it is an invitation for both parties of the conversation to explore where the problem is and how to solve it. Only by tackling the problem can friendship be formed. Indeed, there is no need for criticism if people do not think you are worth it.

So... thank you. I do not think we will ever meet, but I will always cherish the good lessons you have taught me. Best wishes for you future life and career.

Yours Sincerely,

Christine

On Life, Love, Literature & Letter Writing

#27: On "Uneven Ink"

February 27, 2015
To: B.G., Ottawa, Ontario, Canada

Greetings from Australia. What a wonderful letter you have sent me, full of personal observations on the handwritten words and their impact on human lives. I particularly like this paragraph of yours:

"As a former designer and educator, I won't knock the printed word or good typography, electronic or pressed, for its ease, beauty and effectiveness. But I suspect there is little to replace the handwritten letter for capturing the personal."

Indeed, I have been writing with computers since my teenage years. Back in my university days, whenever people handed in pages after pages for assignments, all I produced was a single sheet of nicely printed paper with the font and format that I thought would best capture my character and style. These aspects of my "personal" have changed a bit throughout the years -- for example, I have "migrated" from Times New Roman to Book Antiqua and would occasionally try Garamond, Calibri and even Monotype Corsiva for different and often dramatic writing effects. Handwriting is treated only as a note-taking tool for the sake of speed and convenience, although my handwriting is so lousy that sometimes I have to create a computer file as a reminder of what I have written by hand.

Which is why opportunities such as InCoWriMo are so precious. To me, it is not only a chance to write daily, but also a crucial way to re-familiarise myself with something that has been long lost in my life. While I have developed a sore hand after 26 days of letter writing, my handwriting is considerably improved. It is an interesting process, observing how my thoughts and emotions take shape on paper. While they used to appear on the computer screen almost so quickly that they look like mass-produced products, writing on paper is almost like creating individual and unique art works – you simply cannot go back to correct your mistakes.

You mentioned this special exhibition in Ottawa: "What caught my eye was a document from the mid-1860s outlining and establishing Canada as a country. It wasn't the official decree carefully written by what I suppose to be the national calligrapher number one. No, this was the document written out after one or several meetings by a single hand and signed by the other attendees."

The words that followed are absolutely beautiful: "It was wonderful to see the uneven ink in the radically sharpened nib. The speed of execution of some paragraphs and concentration and pauses in others. Words stroked out and scratched into correctness. It makes my writing have context and those that have written to me. I don't think any photo or copy could have done it justice. I've always worried about refreshing the ink in my pen. No more."

These words of yours touched something deep in me. Talk about capturing the "personal" – is it possible that writing with computers is a way for me to disguise something untidy in me? Immature thoughts, raw emotions, feelings that are too tender to be delivered directly from hand to paper, perhaps. A fear to show these newborn aspects of me leads to a desire to place grown-up masks on them. Therefore, the process of displaying things in print is like an affirmation, a kind of approval from a parent to her kids: "OK, now you've got some clothes on, you can go out."

It leads to the suspicion that we believe in print so much that anything not in print is far from ready. The same way in which self-publishing used to be and probably still is considered by many as being less prestigious than traditional publishing. I wonder to what extent has the simple pleasure of writing as an act been smothered by a writer's efforts to secure a publisher. In this sense, perhaps Amazon.com and other digital publishing platforms have more or less contributed to the revival of the art of letter writing – with publishing becoming something that anybody and everybody can easily do, we no longer need approval from the others to determine the value of our own words. Hence we shift our focus to the words themselves – their texture, their density, their sustenance as part of us, their natural and prolonged existence as representatives of our "personal" being, belonging and becoming. We write, so we are.

The way you use your words – it reveals much about you. I see that you are a born educator, with an eye to and passion for detail, fully capable of transforming abstract concepts into beautiful and inspiring words. I dare to propose that designing is similar in its nature and significance – to convey what is lurking under the surface, something we can sense but are unable to express in images and/or words, and to amplify and advocate for its potential impact on our lives. I look forward to receiving your next letter.

Yours Sincerely,

Christine

#28: The Power of Words

February 28, 2015
To: C.C., Huntsville, Alabama, U.S.A.

    Greetings from Australia. It was a surprise to receive your letter – a nice one indeed. I had been looking forward to hearing from you, but when I received a letter from B about two weeks ago, I assumed that as a couple, you have been sharing your InCoWriMo correspondence list. I remember writing to him something like this: "It is wonderful to know that you both are passionate about letter writing and blogging. This convinces me that you must be sharing a love for reading, too. I think it is one of the best things a man and his wife can do."

    What is the chance of me being chosen by both of you, separately, as husband and wife, as someone to communicate with on the other side of the world? It reminds me of Kahill Gibran's *The Prophet*, in which he writes on marriage:

    "Yes, you shall be together even in the silent memory of God. But let there be spaces in your togetherness. And let the winds of heaven dance between you. Love one another, but make not a bond of love. Let it rather be a moving sea between the shores of your souls... Sing and dance together and be joyous, but each one of you be alone – even as the strings of a lute are alone, though they quiver with the same music... And stand together yet not too near together: For the pillars of the temple stand apart. And the oak tree and the Cyprus grow not in each other's shadows."

And thank you for sharing how you and B have come together. Like you, my husband and I met and became a couple through letter writing. I have always believed in the power of words – they reveal so much about us, like a telescope that pinpoints on a star while helping us to imagine the whole universe. To borrow your words, "honest discussions and sincere exchanges" can lead us to each other's soul.

The power of words also led me to starting my current business. To make a long story short: I have always considered myself lucky, to be able to read and write in both languages. There are so many wonderful books out there that I thought, what if I could do as much as I could to bring these beautiful writings across the linguistic and cultural boundaries? As soon as I found a way to do so, there is no turning back. Money was, is and will continue to be an issue, but I do believe I am working on something useful and worthy of doing.

You asked whether there are ebook readers readily available in Asia. The short answer is no, but things have been changing, though not as fast as what they have been in the West. It frustrates me sometimes, but as they say in that movie *Field of Dreams*, "If you build it, they will come." I just need to be patient.

Translation is indeed very hard. I guess this is difficult for people who have never done it to understand. To me, it is like trying to read a book aloud, word by word, say, J.R.R. Tolkien's *The Lord of the Rings* or all seven of J.K. Rowling's Harry Potter books. There is no surprise that both examples belong to the genre of fantasy – it can be such a wild ride that plenty of imagination and inspiration are required. Imagine you are not just reading the words, but acting them out, giving life to them with sounds, rhythms, facial expressions and body movements, singing them into existence, making them take wing and soar. It is like magic.

And, throughout this process, you are completely alone. It is a journey only you can embark on and complete. No one sees you, understands you and stands by you. You can only persevere in the dark and crawl through one word after another, on your own hands and knees, sometimes bleeding and exhausted. Here I mean no offence, but people who are monolingual cannot fully appreciate the efforts it takes to make the transition between two languages, not to mention the transformation of one culture into another. It is something that no machine can ever do. To take a high-art example: Imagine holding a copy of the painting *Mona Lisa* in your hands. Think of meeting Leonardo Da Vinci himself and seeing him actually creating it – then you will see what I mean.

The only thing that sustains you is the power of words. I suppose it is why we love writing, not just you and B and me, but also the numerous nameless people out there who pick up their pens or turn on their computers every day and night. We write, not so much because we want to escape from something or anything in our lives, but precisely because we want to write ourselves into this world. We want to participate, to communicate, to have our voices heard, but, most importantly, to carefully listen. To borrow Gibran's words above, we want to know we are not the only string on the lute that is the universe. We want to quiver with the same music that is humanity.

I want this last letter I wrote for InCoWriMo 2015 to be for you, because we share something together. You understand how it is to have found not only a love for writing but also the love of your life *through* writing – that is something really special and precious. Which is why I believe the art of letter writing has never been lost – it is us who have found multiple paths to go along towards that final destination of expressing our mutual affection and respect through words. And, in the same way that print books and ebooks should exist in harmony, handwritten letters can and will continue to exist together with emails and blogs. Long live the power of words!

Yours Sincerely,

Christine

(#29: Pretending It's a Leap Year)

February 29, 2015 (?)
To: Constant Reader, Everywhere

My Dear,

    Greetings from Australia. This is not a Leap Year, so there are only 28 letters collected in this little book. However, for the want of a chance to thank you for reading me, I feel like adding one more day to February, just this once. It is a pleasure to have met you in words.

    Let me see if I can introduce myself in exactly 29 words: "Christine Sun is a bilingual writer, translator, reader and independent scholar. Via her website eBook Dynasty, she helps all English-language authors to promote their titles in the Chinese world."

    Having worked with words all my life, for them I have a passion that is bordering addiction. They are my habit and hobby, my career, my lifestyle and lifeline, my survival tool. They are a life-long journey, a world without end, a love that never dies. I am sure you know what I mean – after all, you are here.

    But this is more than just you and me. It is about life, love and literature, and, most importantly, it is about letter writing. I would like to invite you to participate in next year's InCoWriMo, to take up the challenge of writing something by hand each day throughout February – a letter, a postcard, a note, whatever. Send it to someone you know or a complete stranger. Tell them how much you love this world and all the words that were, are and will be in it. Share with them how happy you are to be alive. You think you can do it? Of course you can.

Writing is not hard. You just need to use your heart. As I have said somewhere in this book, I believe the art of letter writing has not been lost. In whatever form you communicate, the key is to be sincere. Even if your handwriting is as lousy as mine, people would love to hear from you and to know that you *care*. This is the magic we can all master – to conjure something beautiful and precious out of nothing. This is what makes us unique – it is words, not wars, that have shaped our world the way it is today. With our writing, we can make it even better.

I should stop now and hand the pen to you. It will be fine if you are into keyboards and/or finger-dancing on tablets, for the act of communicating remains the same. Write a letter, now. After that, you will not want to stop. Trust me.

I wish you all the happiness, health and success for the coming year. See you in February 2016, when the next InCoWriMo begins.

Yours Sincerely,

Christine

On Life, Love, Literature & Letter Writing

About Christine Yunn-Yu Sun:

Born in Taiwan and now based in Melbourne, Australia,
Christine is a bilingual writer, translator, reader, reviewer,
occasional journalist and independent scholar.
She assists emerging and established
English-language authors, literary agents and publishers
to translate, publish and promote their titles
as digital and print books to the Chinese World,
while helping Chinese-language writers
promote their writings to the English World.

On Life, Love, Literature & Letter Writing

Other books by Christine Yunn-Yu Sun:

My Twitter Tiny Little Poems (Book of Bilingual Poetry)

Voices under the Sun: English-Language Writings by Australian and Other Authors with Chinese Ancestry (Literary Criticism)

Journey to the West
The Three Kingdoms
The Water Margin
Dream of the Red Chamber
(English Re-Writing of Chinese Classic Novels for Young Readers)

www.ingramcontent.com/pod-product-compliance
Lightning Source LLC
Chambersburg PA
CBHW071410080526
44587CB00017B/3233